POP CULTURE BIOS

IDINA

MENZEL

VOCAL

HEATH

...blications Company
...Publishing Gr...

Idina Menzel (LEFT) and Kristen Bell (RIGHT) pose for the camera at the 2014 Academy Awards.

INTRODUCTION

Idina pours her heart into a song for a recording.

By 2014, Idina Menzel had been performing as a singer and an actress for more than twenty years. She'd had roles on Broadway and in major films. And now she was about to perform at the Oscars.

"Let It Go," a song her character, Elsa, sings in the movie *Frozen*, was nominated for an Academy Award for Best Original Song. Idina had to sing the song for an audience that included major stars such as Brad Pitt, Meryl Streep, and Julia Roberts. Her performance would be on live television too! She was a little nervous.

Idina Menzel glammed up for the Oscars in 2014.

Idina voiced Elsa in the movie *Frozen*.

Idina knew the song, of course. Still, she had trained hard so her voice would be up to the task. She even practiced the song by performing for fans at a small New York City restaurant.

A few days earlier, she had rehearsed onstage at the Dolby Theatre, in Los Angeles, California. The technology used for the awards show took some getting used to. Idina would be performing her song with an orchestra. But the orchestra would actually be in a different building. A microphone and a monitor helped the songstress and the musicians stay together.

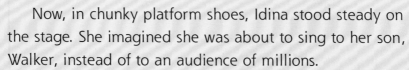

Now, in chunky platform shoes, Idina stood steady on the stage. She imagined she was about to sing to her son, Walker, instead of to an audience of millions.

As the orchestra played the first notes of the song, Idina began singing softly, her voice full of emotion. When she nailed her last note, the captivated crowd stood to applaud.

Idina belts out "Let It Go" at the Oscars.

RISING STAR

Idina was born in Queens, New York.

Idina Kim Menzel was only eight years old when she decided to be a performer. She wanted to play the lead role in the musical *Annie*. But she knew it would take practice to get there. So she went around singing the song "Tomorrow" at full volume.

Idina's parents wanted to make sure she learned how to sing correctly. They began looking for a coach to give her singing lessons.

Taming Her Talent

It didn't take long for Idina's parents to find a voice coach. There was just one problem. The coach they selected didn't normally work with kids. But when she heard Idina sing, she changed her mind.

Idina always wanted to play little orphan Annie.

Idina was born in Queens, New York, on May 30, 1971. She spent most of her childhood in Syosset, Long Island.

As talented as Idina was, she still needed lots of training. Although she had a beautiful voice, her technique needed work. When Idina sang, she'd belt out notes so loudly that she was in danger of harming her throat! The coach wanted to teach Idina how to sing at the right volume and to take care of her voice.

Idina's voice coach changed her fate. Idina learned to sing powerfully but more quietly. She learned to control her breathing. And as the lessons went on, Idina learned how to truly touch people with her voice.

BUDDING STAR

As a fifth grader, Idina played Dorothy in *The Wizard of Oz*. Judy Garland (RIGHT) played the role in the 1939 movie version.

Cover Girl

Idina's voice improved so much that she started singing at weddings and bar mitzvahs when she was a teenager. She sang songs by Whitney Houston, Celine Dion, Barbra Streisand, and other popular artists. By then her parents had divorced. Idina lived with her mother and sister, Cara. The money Idina earned helped to support her family.

BAR MITZVAH = *a celebration held when a Jewish boy turns thirteen to recognize that he has come of age*

Getting paid to sing made Idina a pro. Still, something was missing. She realized she wanted to do more than imitate other singers. She wanted to show off her own style and sing songs no one else had sung before. But she wasn't sure how to move her career in that direction.

As a teen, Idina enjoyed singing songs by gifted vocalist Whitney Houston (ABOVE).

Broadway Bound

After graduating from high school, Idina majored in drama at the Tisch School of the Arts at New York University. Her mom was fine with her choice. But her dad wanted her to work toward a different type of degree. He knew show business was cutthroat and competitive. He worried she wouldn't make it. And if she didn't, she wouldn't be qualified for other jobs when she graduated.

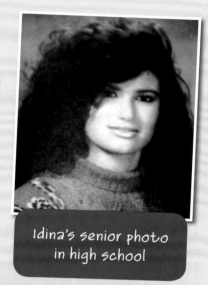

Idina's senior photo in high school

Idina stuck with her plans and earned a bachelor's degree in drama in 1993. After graduating, she kept singing at weddings and bar mitzvahs. But she began auditioning for roles in shows too.

AUDITIONING =
giving a short performance in hopes of being chosen for a part

Idina's family name is Mentzel. People often mispronounced it, not realizing that the *t* was silent. So when she grew up, she changed it.

As her dad had worried, some directors rejected Idina. But getting turned down for a part didn't mean she'd wasted her time. Every audition gave Idina a chance to practice her skills and make connections in show business.

At one audition, a director didn't think she was right for the role. But he thought she'd be great for a different part in a new show called *Rent*.

Idina's audition put her on the path to Broadway. She sang "When a Man Loves a Woman" for the producers of *Rent* and won a lead role as the character Maureen.

Idina and her dad smile for the camera.

13

Idina (FAR RIGHT) and the cast of *Rent* on Broadway

CHAPTER TWO

TAKING THE STAGE

Idina, Taye Diggs, and a third cast member of *Rent*

Idina holds her son, Walker.

In *Rent*, Idina played one of a group of friends struggling to make it in New York City. To make sure she did her best, Idina went back to her vocal coach to train. She sometimes performed eight shows in one week. And she didn't want to wear out her voice.

Rent started as an off-Broadway production. But the show was so popular that it moved to the Nederlander Theatre, a Broadway theater, just two months later.

On April 29, 1996, *Rent* debuted on Broadway—and Idina did too. She was performing for much larger audiences. Critics praised her performance. She was nominated for a Tony Award in 1996.

Idina shows off her Tony nomination.

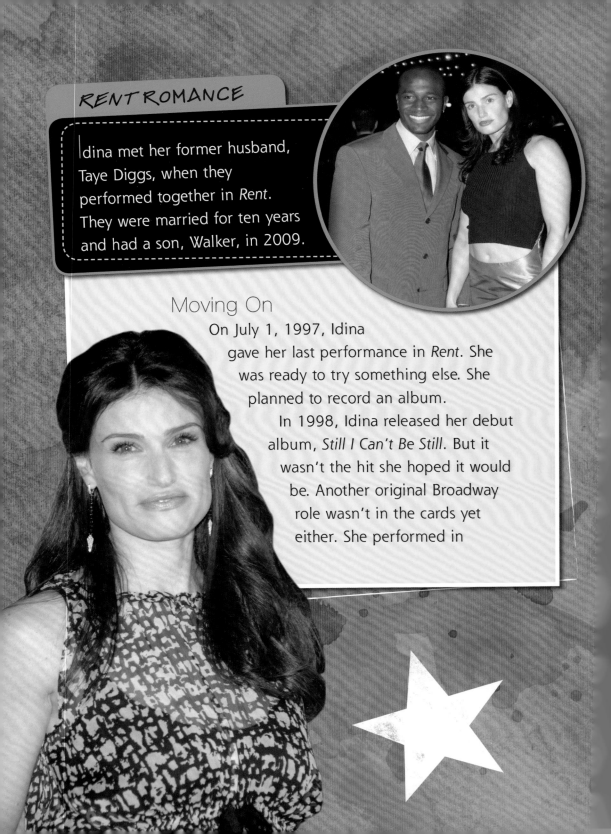

Idina met her former husband, Taye Diggs, when they performed together in *Rent*. They were married for ten years and had a son, Walker, in 2009.

Moving On

On July 1, 1997, Idina gave her last performance in *Rent*. She was ready to try something else. She planned to record an album.

In 1998, Idina released her debut album, *Still I Can't Be Still*. But it wasn't the hit she hoped it would be. Another original Broadway role wasn't in the cards yet either. She performed in

The cast of *Aida* celebrates the show's second year on Broadway.

off-Broadway shows between 1999 and 2001 and was in *Aida* on Broadway in 2000.

Idina had proven herself in *Rent*. But she still felt that nobody really knew who she was. She wasn't famous. And she wasn't getting any more roles in brand-new shows.

Wicked-Awesome Audition

Then came an audition for a new Broadway show called *Wicked*. Idina sang "Defying Gravity." At first, things went fine. But on the very last note, her voice cracked. Idina reacted with a burst of fury. She screamed out a curse word. Then she gave it a second try and nailed the note. But she knew there was no way she'd get the part after that performance.

As it turned out, the director was impressed—by

GOING GREEN

The green makeup Idina wore to play Elphaba took about forty minutes to apply but only ten minutes to remove.

her voice as well as by her wild emotions. In 2000, Idina won the role of Elphaba.

Dedicated Diva

As the wicked witch Elphaba, Idina found huge fame. She gained tons of fans, many of them teenagers. And in 2004, she wasn't just nominated for a Tony Award—she won one!

Idina tearfully thanks the crowd for her Tony.

Although things went very well for Idina in *Wicked*, she did hit one snag. On the night before her last performance, there were technical problems. A platform onstage was lowered too soon. When Idina stepped onto it, she fell. Mid-performance, the show was stopped. An ambulance was called. An understudy took over while Idina was rushed to the hospital.

UNDERSTURY =
a substitute actor

SOARING SONGSTRESS

In *Wicked*, Idina got to "fly" above the audience every night as she performed her favorite song, "Defying Gravity." Idina would rise into the air, supported by a hidden steel platform and belt.

The next day, she showed up at the theater with a cracked rib. The understudy was playing Elphaba, but Idina didn't want to let her fans down. At the end of the show, Idina surprised the audience by performing in the final scene. The audience screamed in appreciation. They gave her a standing ovation.

STANDING OVATION = when an audience stands up and gives long, loud applause to show appreciation for a performance

Idina (CENTER) performs in *If/Then* on Broadway.

CHAPTER THREE

LEADING LADY

Idina (SECOND FROM LEFT) and the voice actors of *Frozen* proudly hold their gold records.

REPRISED =
to play the same role over again

After her success in *Wicked*, Idina had no problem scoring all kinds of projects. In 2004, she released her album *Here*. The next year, she reprised her role as Maureen in the movie version of *Rent*. And in 2008, she released another album called *I Stand*.

Idina played Maureen in both the Broadway and movie versions of *Rent*.

23

Lea Michele (LEFT) and Idina (RIGHT) perform "Poker Face" on the TV show Glee.

Meanwhile, her fans noticed the strong resemblance between her and Lea Michele, star of the TV show Glee. They thought that because the two looked so similar, Idina should play the mother of Lea's character, Rachel.

Glee's producers agreed. In 2010, Idina joined the cast as Shelby Corcoran, Rachel's mother and the coach of a rival high school choir, Vocal Adrenaline.

Disney Dreams

By 2010, Idina's talents were no secret. But that didn't mean she got every part she wanted. When she tried out for the Disney movie Tangled, she hoped for a leading role. Instead, she walked away with nothing.

GIVING BACK

In 2010, Idina founded A BroaderWay summer camp with her then-husband, Taye Diggs. Girls from urban neighborhoods attend the camp to learn and perform.

That wasn't the end of the story, however. Though Idina didn't know it, a casting director had recorded her audition. When Disney began working on a different movie, *Frozen*, the director convinced them Idina was perfect for the main role.

In 2013, Idina starred as the voice of Elsa in *Frozen*. One of her character's songs, "Let It Go," won an Oscar for Best Original Song in 2014. Idina's performance of the song also helped her cross over from stage star to pop radio star.

Kristen Bell (LEFT) and Idina (RIGHT) perform "For the First Time in Forever" at the Los Angeles Vibrato Grill Jazz club.

Idina's dad had nothing to worry about when she majored in drama. Today her parents are two of her biggest fans.

Back to Broadway

By March 2014, Idina was back on Broadway. This time, she was the star of *If/Then*, a new musical about a woman making major changes in her life. She was excited to be in a show that captured her heart. She was also excited to see her name on the sign outside the theater. Idina felt she had a big responsibility for the success—or failure—of the show.

As it turned out, fans could hardly wait for *If/Then* to open. The first seven shows were preview performances. That week, *If/Then* earned nearly $1 million in ticket sales.

Idina (CENTER) and the cast of *If/Then* show off the CD of their cast recording.

Pure Professional

Throughout her career, Idina has proven herself onstage, on television, and on the big screen. She's not afraid to show her talents. And she's not discouraged by challenges. Her hard work and determination keep her in the business she loves.

With a string of popular projects and a ton of adoring fans, Idina seems poised to enjoy success for many years to come.

Idina performs at the Born Free Africa Mother's Day Family Carnival in New York.

ANNIE AFTER ALL

At a live concert in 2012, Idina got her chance to sing "Tomorrow" from the musical *Annie*. Her childhood dream had come true!

IDINA
PICS!

Idina attends the 2013 Olivier Awards in London.

Idina performs at Radio City Music Hall.

Idina gets glammed up for the 2013 Tony Awards.

29

Donovan, Sandy. *Music and Theater Top Tens.*
Minneapolis: Lerner Publication, 2015.
Read more about the stars of the music and theater business.

Idina on Facebook
https://www.facebook.com/IdinaMenzel
Join nearly one million "Fanzels" who "like" Idina too.

Idina on Twitter
https://twitter.com/idinamenzel
Get the latest updates straight from the source.

Idina's Official Site
http://idinamenzel.com
Get connected to Idina's social networking sites through her official site.

If/Then
http://www.ifthenthemusical.com/home
Learn all about Idina's latest show.

Malaspina, Ann. *What's Great about New York?*
Minneapolis: Lerner Publications, 2015.
Learn more about Idina's home state.

INDEX

PHOTO ACKNOWLEDGMENTS

The images in this book are used with the permission of: © Kevin Winter/Getty Images, pp. 2, 5, 7; © AF Archive/Alamy, pp. 3 (top), 23; © Victoria Hurn/Alamy, p. 3 (bottom); © Alberto E. Rodriguez/WireImage/Getty Images, p. 4 (top left); AP Photo/Jordan Strauss/Invision, p. 4 (top right); © Bruce Glikas/FilmMagic/Getty Images, pp. 4 (bottom), 21; AP Photo/Disney, p. 6; © Slaven Vlasic/Getty Images, p. 8 (top left); © Vera Anderson/WireImage/Getty Images, p. 8 (top right); © JTB Media Creation, Inc./Alamy, p. 8 (bottom); © Moviestore collection Ltd/Alamy, p. 9; © Photos 12/Alamy, p. 10; © Peter Bischoff/Getty Images, p. 11; Seth Poppel Yearbook Library, p. 12; © Evan Agostini/Getty Images, pp. 13, 14 (bottom left); AP Photo/Wally Santana, p. 14 (top); Celebrity Juicer/Splash News/Newscom, p. 14 (bottom right); © Catherine McGann/ Getty Images, p. 15; © Paul Smith/Featureflash/Shutterstock.com, p. 16 (bottom); Fred Prouser/ Reuters/Newscom, p. 16 (top); AP Photo/Mark Lennihan, p. 17; © Frank Micelotta/Getty Images, pp. 18, 20; AP Photo/Kathy Willens, p. 19; AP Photo/National Theatre, Joan Marcus, p. 22 (top); © Alberto E. Rodriguez/Getty Images for Disney, pp. 22 (bottom), 25; © FOX/Getty Images, p. 24; © Astrid Stawiarz/Getty Images, p. 26; © Robin Marchant/Getty Images, p. 27; © Victoria Hurn/Alamy, p. 28 (bottom left); © StarMaxWorldwide/ImageCollect, p. 28 (right); AP Photo/Rex Features, p. 28 (top left); © Vera Anderson/Getty Images, p. 29 (bottom); © Naomi Galai/Getty Images, p. 29 (top left); © Walter McBride/WireImage/Getty Images, p. 29 (top middle); © Debby WongShutterstock.com, p. 29 (right).

Front cover: © Kristin Callahan/Ace Pictures/Newscom (large image); © Kevin Winter/Getty Images (small image).

Back cover: © S_buckley/Shutterstock.com.

Main body text set in Shannon Std Book 12/18.
Typeface provided by Monotype Typography.

0500000677949 5

You probably know Idina Menzel as the amazing singer of "Let It Go" and the voice of Elsa in the movie *Frozen*. But did you know that she:

★ dreamed of playing the title character in the musical *Annie*?

★ sang at weddings and bar mitzvahs before making it big on Broadway?

★ started a summer camp for kids?

Want to know more about the life of this singing superstar? Read on to learn all about Idina's road to stardom, Broadway breakthrough, television debut, and more!

POP CULTURE BIOS

T1-AMW-864

ISBN 978-1-4677-6102-4
50795

Lerner Classroom™
A division of Lerner Publishing Group
www.lernerbooks.com
008–012 Guided Reading: R*
*Provided by a trained reading consultant

9 781467 761024